Elephants in Danger

by Helen Orme

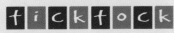

CONTENTS

Words that appear **in bold** are explained in the glossary.

Copyright © **ticktock Entertainment Ltd 2008**
First published in Great Britain in 2008 by **ticktock Media Ltd.**,
Unit 2, Orchard Business Centre, North Farm Road,
Tunbridge Wells, Kent, TN2 3XF
ISBN 978 1 84696 782 5 pbk
Printed in China

We would like to thank Penny Worms, our consultants, The Born Free Foundation – www.bornfree.org.uk and the National Literacy Trust.

Picture credits: t=top, b=bottom, c=centre, l-left, r=right
Corbis: 16bl, 20-21, 22-23, 28t. Shutterstock: OFC, 1, 2, 4-5, 6-7, 8-9, 10-11, 12, 15, 18, 19, 25t, 25c, 26, 27, 28b, 29, 31, 32. Superstock: 11bl, 13, 14, 16-17, 24b.
Every effort has been made to trace the copyright holders, and we apologise in advance for any unintentional omissions. We would be pleased to insert the appropriate acknowledgements in any subsequent edition of this publication.

THE BIGGEST OF THEM ALL

Elephants are the world's largest land-living mammals.

These clever animals live in different **habitats**, from the open **savannahs** of Africa to the forests of Asia.

In Africa, there are even desert elephants.
They are experts at searching for water and food.

ELEPHANT FACT

There are two types of elephant, the African and the Asian.

This picture shows a young Asian elephant.

Elephants have no natural **predators** but life is becoming difficult for them.

AFRICAN ELEPHANTS

Once African elephants lived across the whole of Africa. Now they only live in the areas marked red on the map. African elephants live on open savannahs and in deserts and forests.

AFRICA

There are thought to be over 470,000 elephants in Africa. In some parts, the numbers are increasing but they are under threat from **poaching**, farming and **climate change**.

Both male and female African elephants have tusks.

Young bull (male) elephants practise fighting with their small tusks.

ASIAN ELEPHANTS

*Asian elephants live in forests and open **grasslands** in the parts of Asia marked in red. Some live in mountain regions.*

There are fewer than 50,000 Asian elephants left.

Asian elephants are smaller than African elephants. They have much smaller tusks and ears. Female Asian elephants do not have tusks.

Unlike African elephants, Asian elephants have been used as working animals for thousands of years.

ELEPHANT LIFE

Females and young elephants live in family herds.

Males leave their herd when they are about 13 years old. They live alone, or in **bachelor groups** with other males.

Female elephants are called cows. They start to have calves when they are between 10 and 13 years old.

All the cows in the herd help to look after the babies.

ELEPHANT MUMS

Female elephants are pregnant for 22 months. This is the longest time of any mammal.

This calf has just been born!

FINDING FOOD

Elephants feed on plants, including grass, roots, branches, fruit, tree bark and even farm crops.

They eat a huge amount each day and need a big area to **forage** for food.

Each day an elephant needs to drink around 230 litres of water. They use their tusks to dig in the ground for roots and to find water.

Their digging makes waterholes that other animals can use.

BABY FOOD

A baby elephant drinks its mother's milk using its mouth, not its trunk. Babies start to eat solid food when they are about two years old.

AMAZING TRUNKS

An elephant's trunk is an overgrown nose and lip. At the end it has 'fingers' that can feel an object and pick it up.

Trunks are very useful for lifting food into an elephant's mouth or for sucking up water. A young elephant must learn how to suck up water into its trunk and then pour it into its mouth.

Elephants often use their trunks like a shower to squirt water or dust over their backs.

TUSKS

Tusks are very long teeth. If an elephant loses a tusk it makes it difficult to dig for water or roots.

Baby elephants get their first real tusks when they are about two years old. Before that they grow small 'milk tusks'.

Tusks are made of ivory. This is worth a lot of money.

Hundreds of thousands of elephants have been killed for their tusks.

GIANT TUSK

The largest elephant tusk ever recorded weighed 97 kilograms – the weight of a large man!

A working elephant gives rides to tourists in India.

WORKING ELEPHANTS

Elephants have been used as working animals for thousands of years.

They have been used to carry people, lift heavy loads and pull carts. They have even carried soldiers into war! Nowadays, machines do most of this work.

Looking after retired working elephants can be a problem. The elephants have to live in **sanctuaries** because they cannot look after themselves.

Some tame elephants have been trained to paint pictures! These are sold to raise money.

KILLING ELEPHANTS FOR IVORY

African elephants have always been hunted for food and for their ivory tusks.

Ivory is easy to carve so it was used to make beautiful objects that were worth a lot of money.

It is now against the law to buy or sell new objects made from ivory.

Elephants are protected by law, too, but poachers ignore this.

These tusks have been taken away from poachers. They are burned so they cannot be sold.

A SAFE PLACE TO LIVE

There is another danger to elephants. Their habitat is becoming farmland.

Forest elephants are threatened by **logging**.

Wildlife reserves give elephants a safe place to live but they need huge areas to find enough food and water.

If the reserves are too small, the elephants eat everything and there is not enough time for the plants to grow back.

GLOSSARY

bachelor groups Groups of young male elephants.

climate change When the weather in an area changes and stays changed.

droughts When there is no rain for a very long time.

forage To look for food.

grasslands Dry areas covered with grass where only a few bushes and trees grow.

habitats Places that suit particular wild animals or plants.

logging Cutting down trees for wood.

poaching The illegal capturing or killing of animals.

predators Animals that live by killing and eating other animals.

sanctuaries Safe places for animals that could not survive in the wild.

savannahs Large, open areas of land in Africa where grasses and bushes grow.

tourists People who are on holiday.

wildlife reserves Places set aside for wild animals and plants to live. The animals and their habitat are protected by laws.

INDEX